In Loving Memory

In Loving Memory

In Loving Memory

In Loving Memory

In Loving Memory

In Loving Memory

In Loving Memory

In Loving Memory

In Loving Memory

In Loving Memory

In Loving Memory

In Loving Memory

In Loving Memory

In Loving Memory

In Loving Memory

In Loving Memory

In Loving Memory

In Loving Memory

In Loving Memory

In Loving Memory

In Loving Memory

In Loving Memory

In Loving Memory

In Loving Memory

In Loving Memory

In Loving Memory

In Loving Memory

In Loving Memory

In Loving Memory

In Loving Memory

In Loving Memory

In Loving Memory

In Loving Memory

In Loving Memory

In Loving Memory

In Loving Memory

In Loving Memory

In Loving Memory

In Loving Memory

In Loving Memory

In Loving Memory

In Loving Memory

In Loving Memory

In Loving Memory

In Loving Memory

In Loving Memory

In Loving Memory

In Loving Memory

In Loving Memory

In Loving Memory

In Loving Memory

In Loving Memory

In Loving Memory

In Loving Memory

In Loving Memory

In Loving Memory

In Loving Memory

In Loving Memory

In Loving Memory

In Loving Memory

In Loving Memory

In Loving Memory

In Loving Memory

In Loving Memory

In Loving Memory

In Loving Memory

In Loving Memory

In Loving Memory

In Loving Memory

In Loving Memory

In Loving Memory

In Loving Memory

In Loving Memory

In Loving Memory

In Loving Memory

In Loving Memory

In Loving Memory

In Loving Memory

In Loving Memory

In Loving Memory

In Loving Memory

In Loving Memory

In Loving Memory

In Loving Memory

In Loving Memory

In Loving Memory

In Loving Memory

In Loving Memory

In Loving Memory

In Loving Memory

In Loving Memory

In Loving Memory

In Loving Memory

In Loving Memory

In Loving Memory

In Loving Memory

In Loving Memory

In Loving Memory

In Loving Memory

In Loving Memory

www.ingramcontent.com/pod-product-compliance
Lightning Source LLC
Chambersburg PA
CBHW082106280426
43661CB00090B/903
9781912817030